Snow, sleet, hail or freezing rain, which is which?

snow

freezing rain

1. Snow is made up of star-shaped flakes.
2. Sleet is a mix of snow and rain.
3. Hail is round balls of frozen rain.
4. Freezing rain is liquid rain that freezes when it hits the ground.

Every snowflake forms around a very small speck of dust or pollen. This is one of the things that makes snowflakes different from sleet or hail.

Each snowflake has six arms (or sides), like a hexagon. The shape of the arms depends on how cold it was as the snowflake formed and fell from the cloud. No two snowflakes are the same.

Hexagons have six sides.

You might think that snowflakes are white, but in fact they are clear. They look white because of the way sunlight shines off them.

a mountain in the Alps

Algal blooms, which are a bit like seaweed, can make snow look pink, red or green. Red or pink snow is quite common in the Alps and in Antarctica. Snow can be made yellow or brown by sand, or black by soot, as well.

A blizzard is a snowstorm with very strong winds. It is difficult to see in a blizzard because there is so much snow flying around. At times, the wind picks up snow that is on the ground and blows that around, too. This is called a ground blizzard.

a horse in a blizzard

Sometimes, there is so much snow flying around that it becomes impossible to tell the sky from the ground. This is called a whiteout.

A snow drift is a deep pile of snow. As the wind blows, it picks up dry, powdery snow. The snow is carried on the wind until it hits something in the way, such as a tree, a wall or a house. The snow piles up there.

a house in a snow drift

Snow drifts can be very deep indeed. The biggest snow drift on record was in Gravesend, New York. At 16m deep, it was deeper than a house is tall!

Snow is fun to play and build with. Children (and adults) often build snowmen with it.

If it snows where you live, you can try to build a snow person, too. Make one big ball of snow, and then one or two smaller ones. Stack them one on top of the other, with the biggest one at the bottom. Add stone eyes (/iez/), twig arms and a carrot for the nose.

You can add a hat and a scarf as well.

You might be surprised to learn that we are not the only animals that like playing in the snow or having snowball fights. Japanese macaques (/mu**caks**/) do this, too!

This macaque has made a snowball.

This macaque is eating the snow.

Snow is very slippery. This means that it can be difficult to walk and drive in the snow.

However, it does mean that we can do winter sports, such as skiing (/**skee**ing/), snowboarding and sledding, which all involve skimming over the snow.

Alpine (or downhill) skiing involves going down a mountain.

Nordic (or cross-country) skiing happens on flat snow.

Snowboarding was invented in 1965. The first snowboard was made from two skis (/skeez/) stuck together!

Sledding is sometimes called sledging (/**sle**jing/).

Sledders ride a flat sled down a hill. Sleds are sometimes dragged across the snow by husky dogs.

Some parts of the planet are snowy all of the time. The Arctic, the Antarctic, and the tops of high mountains are never without snow.

You might think that the tops of mountains should be hotter than the rest of the planet because they are closer to the Sun, but in fact they are much colder.

The peak of Mount Everest has snow all of the time.

Often, animals that live on mountain tops, in the Arctic, or in Antarctica have white fur or feathers. This helps them to blend into the snowy landscape.

a snow leopard

Snow leopards live in the mountains of Pakistan and Afghanistan, and in the Himalayas. They have a black and white mottled (spotty) coat, which helps them to blend into the rocks and snow of the mountain tops.

Some parts of the planet have snow in winter but not in summer. The animals that live here sometimes have brown fur or feathers in summer and white fur or feathers in winter. This means that they blend into the background in all seasons, which makes it less likely that they will be caught by a predator (an animal that eats other animals).

summer feathers

winter feathers

This bird, called a rock ptarmigan, has brown feathers in summer and white ones in winter.

Collared lemmings, Arctic foxes and some breeds of weasels and stoats grow a white winter coat, too.

This is an Arctic fox in summer. It has a thin brown coat.

This is an Arctic fox in winter. It has a thick white coat.

This is an ermine in winter. It is difficult to see it in the snow.

Hailstones form in thunderstorm clouds.

thunderstorm clouds

Hailstones are normally smaller than a pea, but they can sometimes be very big indeed. The biggest hailstone ever recorded was over 20cm wide. That is about the same size as a volleyball!

Another enormous hailstone fell in Bangladesh in 1986. It was one kilogram (about the same as a small melon). No other hailstone has ever been that heavy.

Even much smaller, lighter hailstones can cause harm.

This car's roof was dented by a hailstorm of stones around 5cm wide.

When it is snowing and cold outside, it is important to layer up before going out.

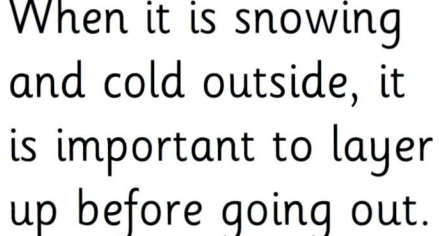

Put on woollen hats, scarves, mittens, snow boots and thick winter coats.

Some dogs need to wrap up to have fun in the cold and snow, too!